Nursery Stencils

❤❤❤❤

Nursery Stencils

Over 20 irresistible designs for everything from
furniture to fabrics

Juliet Moxley

EBURY PRESS
LONDON

For Diana Holstrom, a true friend

First published in 1994

1 3 5 7 9 10 8 6 4 2

Text copyright ©Juliet Moxley 1994
Photographs copyright ©Ebury Press 1994

Juliet Moxley has asserted her right under the Copyright, Designs and Patents Act, 1988
to be identified as the author of this work.

First published in the United Kingdom in 1994 by
Ebury Press
Random House, 20 Vauxhall Bridge Road, London SW1V 2SA

Random House Australia (Pty) Limited
20 Alfred Street, Milsons Point, Sydney, New South Wales 2061, Australia

Random House New Zealand Limited
18 Poland Road, Glenfield, Auckland 10, New Zealand

Random House South Africa (Pty) Limited
PO Box 337, Bergvlei, South Africa

Random House UK Limited Reg. No. 954009

A CIP catalogue record for this book is available from the British Library.

ISBN 0 09 179080 8

Edited by Emma Callery
Photographed by Marie-Lou Avery
Styling by Gloria Nicol
Designed and typeset by Christine Wood

Printed and bound in Portugal by Printer Portuguesa L.d.a.

CONTENTS

INTRODUCTION

♥♥♥♥

Stencilling is a terrific way of personalizing a shop-bought object and making it into something unique, and this book is full of ideas which do just that. Apart from the cot on page 38 which was revamped for a newish baby, all the items used in the book were bought from department stores.

There are ideas here for you to stencil a room, or just the things in it. There are stencils for clothes and furniture, as well as accessories such as a wall light or nursery mat.

I hope you like the wrap-around jacket with four stencils ready for you to use without even having to cut them out. The pig on the front and the hare on the back are featured inside the book too (see pages 64 and 82), and the teddy and ship on the jacket flaps are extras for you to use in whatever way you choose. If you want to use them the same size as they appear on the jacket prepare them with two coats of an oil-based paint first. This prevents them from becoming too soggy with paint and so unusable.

A variety of paints and materials have been used when making this book. All were easy to use and the end results are very colourful - just right for any nursery. I hope that you will find the ideas fun and entertaining and that you enjoy using the book as much as I did creating it.

Juliet Moxley

RIGHT: *The Little Boat curtains. See page 69 for making this stencil*

MATERIALS AND TECHNIQUES

❤❤❤❤

The skills and materials required for stencilling are few, but it is worth practising them before stencilling a treasured possession or freshly painted wall. While it is always possible to paint over a stencil which has gone wrong or which you don't like colourwise, say, a bit of time spent in advance preparing yourself has to be worth it.

BASIC MATERIALS

Stencils

Stencils may be made from a variety of materials including plastic sheet, paper, waxed or manila paper and clear acetate. Metal stencils are used in commercial production and traditionally manila paper was used. Today, however, the most popular material for making stencils is clear acetate. It has the advantage of being transparent so it makes registering the design very easy. It is a flexible material and so will bend round curved surfaces, for example, the hare on the lamp shade featured on page 82. If properly looked after, a stencil should last for years.

Another clear material for making stencils is low-tack peel which is very good if you want to stencil on to cups, plates, or any other form of china. This film closely adheres to the surface and so prevents paint from seeping underneath the stencil.

Permanent marker

You will need this if you are using clear acetate so that you can clearly and easily draw your stencil design on to it.

Craft knife

A craft knife with a sharp point is the best thing to use for cutting stencils. Cutting blades should be fine and never heavy duty. Hold the craft knife as you would a pen and cut towards you with your free hand turning the stencil as you go.

Move the stencil and try to cut continuously so as not to break the line. If you make any mistakes, mend these with clear adhesive tape on either side of the stencil.

Cutting board or mat

Acetate may be cut on a sheet of plain glass approximately 6mm (¼in) thick. A good investment if you are intending to make a lot of stencils is a self-healing mat which has a surface which closes up immediately after cutting. The only drawback to such a mat is that the craft knife tends to drag on this more than it does on glass. An old drawing board may also be used for cutting on.

Masking tape

This is essential both when preparing your stencil (see overleaf) and to fix the stencil in place on the surface you will be covering.

PREPARING BACKGROUNDS

A variety of fine or medium grades of sand-paper are useful for preparing wooden and other rough surfaces, or if you wish to break up a varnished surface, as in the Floral Folk Art blanket box featured on page 32.

Untreated woods should then be primed and undercoated. If you wish to stencil on to raw wood it is best to stain or seal it first.

Before stencilling on to fabric, wash the finish out of it.

PAINTS

Acrylic paints

These are probably the most versatile of paints and they are quick drying. Acrylic paints can be applied to most surfaces but they aren't suitable to use on the top of glossy surfaces. They come in a variety of bright colours and give a glossy rich finish.

Stencil crayons

The many oil-based stencil crayons which are now available are a wonderful invention enabling the most nervous of stencillers to stencil on to a wall without fear of the colour running. To use these, break the seal off the end of the crayon by rubbing it on to rough paper. Then rub the crayon on to a corner of the stencil and rub a stencil brush in the colour. Use a circular movement to transfer the colour from the brush through the stencil. Colours may be blended, but a fresh brush should be used for each colour to prevent them from looking muddy.

Fabric paints

There are many fabric pens and paints, and puff, glitter, and plastic paints on the market, most of which may be used for stencilling. When stencilling a fabric, wash and iron it first and then tape it to a board over some newspaper before starting to stencil. When the colour is dry, the most common way to fix the cloth so that it may be washed is to iron it on the back. Check what the manufacturer's instructions say.

Emulsion paints

Emulsion may be used for stencilling, as used in many of the projects in this book. To protect your stencils, cover them with a coat of clear polyurethane varnish.

Eggshell paints

These are suitable for stencilling on to wooden surfaces only.

APPLYING THE COLOUR

When working with stencils, colour may be applied in many ways. It is best to apply a little colour at a time as most of the mistakes in stencilling are due to using too much paint which then seeps underneath the stencil.

Stencil brushes

The most popular way of applying paint is to use a stencil brush. This is a flat-headed brush. They come in a variety of sizes and grades, they come with long or short handles, and they can be made of synthetic or natural materials. If possible, use one brush per colour; it makes life much easier.

Always clean your brushes thoroughly after use. Use turpentine for oil-based colours, acrylics and varnish, water for fabric and emulsion paints. Or if you are using one brush and want to change colours, a thorough clean - is necessary too.

Sponges

These are also used to apply colour and are ideal when using a large open design. A sponge may also be used to make a mottled area of colour, as in the Ducks and Ducklings mural on page 74.

USING THE STENCILS IN THIS BOOK

You can either trace over each design and use it the size it is, or you can enlarge or reduce it on a photocopier. Alternatively, you can make a grid and place it over the stencil in the book and then transfer the stencil on to a larger or smaller grid, transferring one square at a time.

REVERSING A STENCIL

A stencil may be reversed or flipped to create a mirror image. If you are going to do this, make sure that you clean all the paint off what was the front of the stencil using turpentine and that it is dry. Remember this cannot be done with a stencil which includes numbers or letters.

MAKING AND APPLYING A STENCIL

❤❤❤❤

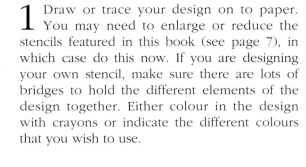

1 Draw or trace your design on to paper. You may need to enlarge or reduce the stencils featured in this book (see page 7), in which case do this now. If you are designing your own stencil, make sure there are lots of bridges to hold the different elements of the design together. Either colour in the design with crayons or indicate the different colours that you wish to use.

2 Lay a piece of acetate over the design and fix in place with masking tape. Using a permanent marker, trace over the part or parts of the design to be stencilled in one colour. Also trace an element or two from the other coloured areas to act as positional guides. Repeat with each of the other colours in the design, each time using a new piece of acetate. If the different coloured elements of the design aren't too close together, or if you are using several stencil brushes, you may choose to use just one piece of acetate for your stencil.

3 Fix the first sheet of acetate to a cutting board with masking tape. Using a very sharp craft knife or scalpel, cut away the areas where the colour is going to be applied remembering not to cut away the positional outlines. Repeat with each sheet of acetate to be used in the stencil.

4 Fix the first sheet of acetate in place with masking tape. Dip the stencil brush (or sponge) in the paint, dab off any excess on to a spare piece of paper or fabric, and then apply the paint with a dabbing motion on to the object which is being stencilled.

When no more colour comes from the brush, dip it into the paint again and repeat as before. If you are using stencil crayons, rub some of the colour on to a spare piece of acetate and dip the stencil brush into this. Repeat with each sheet of acetate ensuring you line them up correctly and use a different brush for each colour or wash thoroughly between colours.

Stencilling
Furniture

DUCKS AND HEARTS

♥♥♥♥

Here is a simple design featuring a stylized duck, heart and waves which has been used to decorate a pretty doll's crib. The same design could also be used on a frieze or on any piece of nursery furniture.

MATERIALS

WOODEN DOLL'S CRIB

SANDPAPER (FINE GRADE)

WOOD PRIMER

PAINTBRUSH

UNDERCOAT

EMULSION PAINT (MAGNOLIA)

ACETATE

PERMANENT MARKER

CRAFT KNIFE

CUTTING BOARD

MASKING TAPE

TAPE MEASURE OR RULER

STENCIL CRAYONS (YELLOW, ORANGE, RED, BLUE)

STENCIL BRUSHES

TURPENTINE

CLEAR POLYURETHANE VARNISH

1 Prepare the crib by rubbing it down with the sandpaper, then paint with wood primer and leave to dry. Paint with undercoat and leave to dry. Finally, paint with the emulsion and once more leave to dry.

2 Trace and alter the size of the stencil given overleaf as appropriate (see page 9). Transfer on to clear acetate and prepare the stencil as described on pages 10-11.

3 Measure the length of the crib and arrange the stencil centrally on one side, repeating the motifs as necessary. Fix the stencil in place with masking tape.

4 Apply the first colour, rubbing the stencil crayon on to a spare piece of acetate. Pick up some of the colour on a stencil brush, and then carefully dab the colour off the brush through the stencil on to the crib. When the first colour is applied, repeat with the other three colours - use a fresh brush for each one, or meticulously wash the brush in turpentine between colours.

5 Repeat steps 3 and 4 on each side of the crib and inside the headboard then leave the colours to set which will take about three days. Mark the duck's eyes with a pencil.

6 Once dry, paint the crib with a coat of clear polyurethane varnish.

VARYING THE DESIGN

You can, of course, just use a single element of the design or vary the position of each part. Stencil a heart on the inside of the headboard in the centre and just above the pillow. Or how about stencilling just the ducks around the edge, each one swimming in the same direction?

ARTIST'S BRUSHES

❤❤❤❤

Do you have problems keeping pencils, paintbrushes and paints tidy? A neat idea to overcome this is to keep them in a large box and what better way to decorate it than with a paintbrush and an image of dripping or splashing paint.

MATERIALS

WOODEN BOX

SANDPAPER (FINE GRADE)

WOOD PRIMER

PAINTBRUSH

UNDERCOAT

EMULSION PAINT (2 SHADES OF BLUE)

ACETATE

PERMANENT MARKER

CRAFT KNIFE

CUTTING BOARD

MASKING TAPE

ACRYLIC PAINTS (4 COLOURS)

STENCIL BRUSHES

GOLD PEN

TURPENTINE

CLEAR POLYURETHANE VARNISH

1 Prepare the box by rubbing it down with the sandpaper, then paint with wood primer and leave to dry. Paint with undercoat and leave to dry. Finally, paint the lid with very pale blue emulsion paint and the base with a slightly darker blue and once more leave to dry.

2 Trace and alter the size of the stencils given overleaf as appropriate (see page 9). You may decide to use just one of the brushes and group of paint blobs, or perhaps several – the choice is yours. Transfer on to clear acetate and prepare the stencils as described on pages 10-11. For this design you will need two pieces of acetate:
● for the paintbrush
● for the paint drips and blobs.

3 Mark the positions for the brush to be stencilled on the lid of the box. Position the stencil, fix it in place with masking tape and then paint the brushes one by one using stencil brushes. Let the first brush dry before stencilling the second one beside it. I painted the handles red and blue, the brushes brown and black, and then used a gold pen for the metallic parts, but you may want to use other colours that you already have. Use a fresh stencil brush for each colour, or meticulously wash the brush in turpentine between colours.

4 The blobs and splashes are stencilled on from the lid down the sides of the box. I used the same shades of red and blue for these.

5 When all the designs are dry, paint the box with a coat of clear polyurethane varnish.

20

Stencil 1 The paintbrush
Stencil 2 The paint drips and blobs

21

TEDDIES JUGGLING

♥♥♥♥

With this design, a pine coffee table was transformed into a child's table. By giving it a coat of creamy white satin wood paint and decorating it with a sweet teddy design using stencil crayons the end result is perfect for any child to play at.

MATERIALS

PINE COFFEE TABLE

SANDPAPER (FINE GRADE)

WOOD PRIMER

PAINTBRUSH

UNDERCOAT

SATIN WOOD PAINT (CREAM OR WHITE)

ACETATE (3 PIECES)

PERMANENT MARKER

CRAFT KNIFE

CUTTING BOARD

MASKING TAPE

STENCIL CRAYONS (RED, BLUE, BROWN)

STENCIL BRUSHES

TURPENTINE

CLEAR POLYURETHANE VARNISH

1 Prepare the table by rubbing it down with the sandpaper, then paint with wood primer and leave to dry. Paint with undercoat and leave to dry. Finally, paint with the satin wood paint and once more leave to dry.

2 Trace and alter the size of the stencils given overleaf as appropriate (see page 9). You may choose to use just one pair, or both. It depends on your design requirements.Transfer on to clear acetate and prepare the stencils as described on pages 10-11. For this design you will need three pieces of acetate:

● for the teddies
● for the teddy details
● for the juggling balls and border.

3 Mark the centre of the table and place the juggling teddies stencil in the middle. Fix in place with masking tape. Using the stencil crayons as described on page 9, stencil one teddy in red and one in blue. Use a fresh stencil brush for each colour, or meticulously wash the brush in turpentine between colours.

4 When the teddies have dried, place the teddy details stencil on top of them and stencil on the markings using the brown stencil crayon.

5 Stencil the juggling balls, and then a border pattern of balls in blue and red around the edge of the table.

6 Leave the colours to set for about three days. Then, if the table is going to come in for hard wear and tear, give it a coat of clear polyurethane varnish.

MAKING A JUGGLING TEDDIES FRIEZE

Pencil positional guides at regular intervals along plain border paper and then stencil the teddies as described above. Add the ball borders along the top and bottom of the strip and, hey presto!, a lively frieze.

Stencil 1 The teddies
Stencil 2 The teddy details
Stencil 3 The juggling balls and border

24

STEAM TRAIN

♥♥♥♥

This small toy box is useful for when you need the odd toy to amuse your child in a room not usually designated for children or for when you are travelling.

MATERIALS

WOODEN BOX

SANDPAPER (FINE GRADE)

UNDERCOAT

PAINTBRUSH

WOOD PRIMER

EMULSION PAINTS (LIGHT BLUE, RED)

ACETATE (3 PIECES)

PERMANENT MARKER

CRAFT KNIFE

CUTTING BOARD

MASKING TAPE

ACRYLIC PAINTS (BLUE, GREEN, RED)

STENCIL BRUSHES

TURPENTINE

CLEAR POLYURETHANE VARNISH

1 Prepare the box by rubbing it down with the sandpaper, then paint with wood primer and leave to dry. Paint with undercoat and then leave to dry thoroughly.

2 Paint the top of the lid and the outside of the base with blue emulsion paint. Leave to dry. Then paint the sides of the lid in red and leave to dry, and finally paint the insides of both top and bottom red and leave to dry once more.

3 Trace and alter the size of the stencil given overleaf as appropriate (see page 9). Transfer on to clear acetate and prepare the stencils as described on pages 10-11. For this design you will need three pieces of acetate:

● for the blue parts of the train and the star
● for the green parts of the train
● for the red parts of the train.

4 Place the stencil for the blue parts of the train and the star on the lid of the box and fix in place with masking tape. Stencil using blue acrylic paint.

5 When the paint is dry, stencil the green parts of the train and when that is dry use the third stencil to apply the red parts. Use a fresh stencil brush for each colour, or meticulously wash the brush in turpentine between colours.

6 Use the same star to stencil red stars on the sides of the box.

7 When all the designs are dry, protect the box with a coat of clear polyurethane varnish.

VARYING THE DESIGN

This steam train would look marvellous chugging around the edges of the box - one on each side - and the stars could adorn the lid painted in several bright colours. Perhaps you might design a carriage to follow the engine around the box, and puffing steam clouds would be great fun coming out of the chimney and over the top of the box.

Stencil 1 The blue parts of the train and the star

Stencil 2 The green parts of the train

Stencil 3 The red parts of the train

SOCK BOX

♥♥♥♥

The items most usually lost in this household are socks and I have found that a set of miniature drawers like this one is just the thing to overcome this particular problem. Decorated in soft shades of emulsion paint, the socks are stencilled on to each drawer.

MATERIALS

WOODEN DRAWERS

SANDPAPER (FINE GRADE)

WOOD PRIMER

PAINTBRUSH

UNDERCOAT

EMULSION PAINTS (VARIOUS COLOURS)

ACETATE (4 PIECES)

PERMANENT MARKER

CRAFT KNIFE

CUTTING BOARD

MASKING TAPE

STENCIL BRUSHES

TURPENTINE

CLEAR POLYURETHANE VARNISH

1 Prepare the box and drawers by rubbing them down with the sandpaper, then paint with wood primer and leave to dry. Paint with undercoat and leave to dry. Finally, paint the box (I used pink) and then each drawer individually (I used shades of soft greens and mauves).

2 Trace and alter the size of the stencils given overleaf as appropriate (see page 9). Transfer on to clear acetate and prepare the stencils as described on pages 10-11. For these socks you will need four pieces of acetate:
● for the main sock motifs
● for the cuff, heel and toe patterns
● for the stars and lines patterns
● for the stripes.

3 Place the main sock stencil on the front edge of the drawer. This is done most easily by taking out the drawer and placing it so that the front face is uppermost. Fix the stencil in place with masking tape and stencil the basic sock shape using a colour in contrast to the drawer colour.

4 Depending on the design you want on your sock, place the correct pattern on top of the sock shape when it is dry. Stencil the cuff, heel and toe, star and lines or the stripes design using different coloured paints (these will look best if you use a darker colour because then the main sock colour won't show through). Use a fresh stencil brush for each colour, or meticulously wash the brush in turpentine between colours.

5 If you want dots on any of your socks, paint these in free hand.

6 When all the designs are dry, paint each drawer and the box surround with a coat of clear polyurethane varnish.

Stencil 1 The main sock motifs
Stencil 2 The cuff, heel & toe patterns
Stencil 3 The stars & lines patterns
Stencil 4 The stripes

FLORAL FOLK ART

❤❤❤❤

This distressed folk art blanket box started life as a highly varnished pine box but the baby's room for which it was designed called for an altogether softer, prettier look. So it was gently distressed and then decorated with a folk art design of flowers and hearts.

MATERIALS

WOODEN BLANKET BOX

SANDPAPER (COARSE GRADE)

EMULSION PAINT (PALE BLUE)

LARGE PAINTBRUSH

ACETATE (5 PIECES)

PERMANENT MARKER

CRAFT KNIFE

CUTTING BOARD

MASKING TAPE

STENCIL CRAYONS (GREEN, BLUE, PINK, YELLOW)

STENCIL BRUSHES

TURPENTINE

CLEAR POLYURETHANE VARNISH

1 Prepare the chest by rubbing it down with coarse sandpaper. This will break up the varnish and allow the emulsion paint to be applied in a patchy fashion.

2 Using a decorator's large paintbrush, give the chest a coat of pale blue emulsion paint. If the paint slides off, wait for it to dry and then sand the surface yet again and paint once more leaving patches of the pine showing through.

3 Trace and alter the size of the stencils given overleaf and on pages 36-7 as appropriate (see page 9). Use as few or as many of the motifs at a time, depending on your design. Transfer on to clear acetate and prepare the stencils as described on pages 10-11. For this design you will need five pieces of acetate:

● for the border (green and blue elements)
● for the border pink flowers
● for the hearts
● for the flower bouquets (green, blue and yellow elements)
● for the bouquet pink flowers.

4 Place the border stencil on the front panels of the chest, fixing in place with masking tape, and apply the colours using the stencil crayons and brushes. Repeat as desired around the sides and on the lid of the chest. Leave to dry. Use a fresh stencil brush for each colour, or meticulously wash the brush in turpentine between colours. Apply the border pink flowers in the same way.

5 Stencil the hearts in pink between the border patterns.

6 Stencil the flower bouquet in the centre of each panel and on the lid of the blanket chest. Leave to dry.

7 Then place the second stencil over the first part of the design and stencil the rest of the design in pink on to the bouquet. Leave the colours to set which will take about three days and then paint the box with a coat of clear polyurethane varnish.

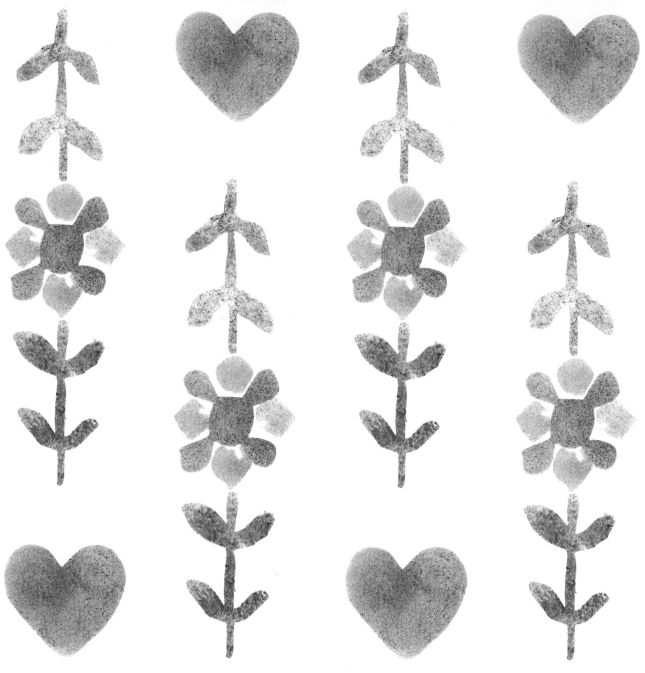

Stencil 1 The border (green & blue elements)
Stencil 2 The border pink flowers

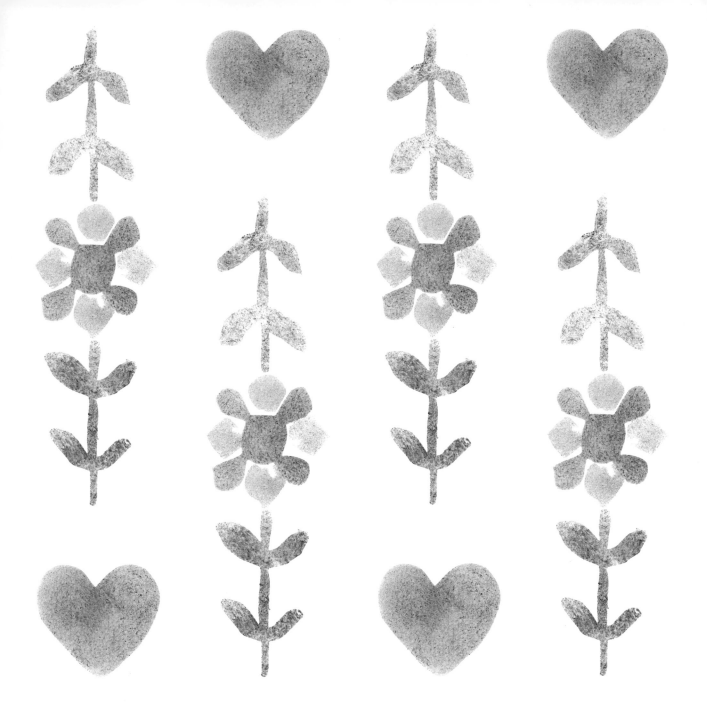

Stencil 3 The hearts

Stencil 4 The flower bouquets (green, blue and yellow elements)
Stencil 5 The bouquet pink flowers

HEARTS AND FLOWERS

♥♥♥♥

This cot was given a new lease of life with some green paint and a folk art stencil. The stencil is a hearts and flower design, slightly more abstract than the one used on the blanket box (see page 32), but the same border pattern (see stencils on pages 36-7 and instructions on page 32) was used to decorate the cot's upright panels.

MATERIALS

COT

SANDPAPER (FINE GRADE)

EMULSION PAINT (PALE GREEN)

LARGE PAINTBRUSH

ACETATE (4 PIECES)

PERMANENT MARKER

CRAFT KNIFE

CUTTING BOARD

MASKING TAPE

STENCIL CRAYONS (GREEN, BLUE, PINK, RED)

STENCIL BRUSHES

TURPENTINE

MATT POLYURETHANE VARNISH

1 Prepare the cot by rubbing down with the sandpaper the areas that you intend to paint (I painted the ends and thicker bars of the sides). This creates a smooth surface on which to apply the emulsion paint.

2 Trace and alter the size of the stencils given overleaf and the border which appears on pages 34-5 as appropriate (see page 9). Use one or both motifs, depending on your design needs. Transfer on to clear acetate and prepare the stencils as described on pages 10-11. For this stencil you will need four pieces of acetate:
● for the border (green and blue elements)
● for the border pink flowers
● for the leaf and heart design
● for the leaf and heart details (red swirls).

3 Place the first border stencil vertically on the cot uprights, fixing it in place with masking tape, and apply the colour using the stencil sticks and brushes (I chose pink for the flowers and green for the leaves). Repeat as necessary down the uprights and leave to dry. Use a fresh stencil brush for each colour, or meticulously wash the brush in turpentine between colours.

4 Using the pink stencil crayon, apply the border details over the existing stencil.

5 Stencil the leaf and heart pattern to the centre of each cot end, both inside and out. Again, I used blue, green and pink for this motif. Leave to dry.

6 Place the second stencil over the first and stencil the rest of the design in red.

7 Leave the colours to set for about three days and then finish off with a coat of clear polyurethane varnish.

Stencil 1 The border (green & blue elements)

Stencil 2 The border pink flowers

Stencil 3 The leaf & heart design

Stencil 4 The leaf & heart details (red swirls)

CAT ON A CHAIR

♥♥♥♥

Where does your cat curl up and go to sleep? On the nearest and most comfortable chair. This cat is permanently on this small chair.

MATERIALS

WOODEN CHAIR

SANDPAPER (FINE GRADE)

WOOD PRIMER

PAINTBRUSH

UNDERCOAT

EMULSION PAINT (PALE BLUE)

ACETATE (2 PIECES)

PERMANENT MARKER (BLACK)

CRAFT KNIFE

CUTTING BOARD

MASKING TAPE

ACRYLIC PAINTS (YELLOW, ORANGE)

STENCIL BRUSHES

TURPENTINE

CLEAR POLYURETHANE VARNISH

1 Prepare the chair by rubbing it down with the sandpaper, then paint with wood primer and leave to dry. Paint with undercoat and leave to dry. Finally, paint with the pale blue emulsion paint and once more leave to dry.

2 Trace and alter the size of the stencils given overleaf as appropriate (see page 9). Use one or both of the cats, depending on your design.

Transfer on to clear acetate and prepare the stencil as described on pages 10-11. For this design you will need two pieces of acetate:
- for the cat outline
- for the markings.

3 Place the cat outline stencil on the seat of the chair and fix in place with masking tape. Stencil the body of the cat in yellow acrylic paint. Leave to dry.

4 Put the second piece of acetate on top of the outline and then stencil on the markings using orange acrylic paint. Use a fresh stencil brush for each colour, or meticulously wash the brush in turpentine between colours. Remove the stencil and draw the eye on the cat using the black permanent marker. ′

5 Wrap masking tape round the legs and the back uprights and stencil orange on the parts which are revealed. Leave to dry and remove the masking tape.

6 Rip more masking tape into thin strips and use them to form triangles on the cross bracings of the chair. Stencil the orange triangle cat markings. As before, leave to dry and then remove the masking tape.

7 Leave all the colours to set which will take about three days and then paint the chair with a coat of clear polyurethane varnish.

Stencil 1 The cat outline
Stencil 2 The markings

44

Stencilling
Fabrics
♥♥♥

STARS AND STRIPES

❤❤❤❤

These inexpensive vests came from my local supermarket - easy to stencil, they make great presents. As well as making colourful vests, these stars look great on T-shirts too.

MATERIALS

VEST

ACETATE (2 PIECES)

PERMANENT MARKER

CRAFT KNIFE

CUTTING BOARD

MASKING TAPE

CARDBOARD

FABRIC FELT-TIPPED PENS (2 COLOURS)

PEARLIZED PUFF PAINTS (2 COLOURS)

1 Trace and alter the size of the stencil given overleaf as appropriate (see page 9). Transfer on to clear acetate and prepare the stencils as described on pages 10-11. For this design, you will need two pieces of acetate:
● for the outline of the star
● for the swirling details.

2 Slide a piece of cardboard between the front and back of the vest to prevent the stencilling colours passing through to the back. Alternatively, use sheets of newspaper cut or folded to the right size, and slide these between the front and back in the same way. Ensure the vest is smooth and fix in place with masking tape.

3 Position the star outline stencil on the front of the vest, again fixing it in place with masking tape, and use a fabric felt-tipped pen to colour the background. Remove the stencil and leave the vest to dry.

4 Position the swirling details stencil and apply the second fabric felt-tipped pen colour. Remove the stencil and leave to dry again.

5 Using the puff paints, dot around the edge of the star shape and over the swirling patterns.

6 Add the finishing touch of dots around the sleeve, bottom and neck edgings.

VARYING THE DESIGN

The size of the stencil can so easily be altered that you might decide to stencil more than one star on to your vest. For example, how about a group of small stars in the bottom corner, or additional stars on each sleeve?

You needn't just stick to clothing either - a galaxy of stars of all sizes on the nursery ceiling would keep you busy. Think about varying their centres too.

Stencil 1 The outline of the star

Stencil 2 The swirling details

SOFT SHOE SHUFFLE

♥♥♥♥

This simple bar strap shoe makes a charming image for a shoe bag. The design has been printed on a panel of white and then appliquéd on to a gingham background.

MATERIALS

PIECE OF WHITE MATERIAL

ACETATE (3 PIECES)

PERMANENT MARKER

CRAFT KNIFE

CUTTING BOARD

MASKING TAPE

NEWSPAPER

FABRIC PAINTS (3 COLOURS)

REVERSING STENCILS

By reversing a stencil you neatly get a mirror image. Do remember to thoroughly clean and dry the stencil before using it flipped, though. With this design, you can now make a neat pair of shoes to adorn the shoe bag; or perhaps you could make a path of shoes across the nursery floor - and up the wall?

1 Trace and alter the size of the stencil given overleaf as appropriate (see page 9). Transfer on to clear acetate and prepare the stencils as described on pages 10-11. For this design you will need three pieces of acetate:
● for the shoe outline
● for the sole
● for the lining and star.

2 Fix the fabric in place with masking tape on a work surface covered with newspaper and then position the first piece of acetate in the centre to make the shoe outline. Dab through a fabric paint and leave to dry.

3 Repeat for the sole, and lining and star stencils, leaving each colour to dry before stencilling on the next. Decorate the star with small dots in a contrasting colour. Use a fresh stencil brush for each colour, or meticulously wash the brush in water between colours.

4 When all the colours are dry, turn the fabric over and iron on the back to fix the paints.

5 Stitch the motif on to, say, a shoebag. Repeat the image for the other side of the bag if you wish.

Stencil 1 The shoe outline
Stencil 2 The sole
Stencil 3 The lining and star

SANDY BUCKETS

❤❤❤❤

Reminiscent of childhood holidays, what could be sweeter than a child's bucket, stencilled in three colours, on to a quilt cover?

MATERIALS

QUILT COVER

ACETATE (3 PIECES)

PERMANENT MARKER

CRAFT KNIFE

CUTTING BOARD

MASKING TAPE

NEWSPAPER

FABRIC PAINTS (3 COLOURS FOR EACH BUCKET)

STENCIL BRUSHES

1 Trace and alter the size of the stencil given overleaf as appropriate (see page 9). Use one or both of the motifs, depending on your design needs. Transfer on to clear acetate and prepare the stencils as described on pages 10-11. For this design you will need three pieces of acetate:
● for the main bucket and rim
● for the handle
● for the bucket's contents

2 Put a piece of newspaper between the layers of the quilt cover to prevent the paint passing through from the front to the back.

3 Use masking tape to keep the quilt cover flat and then mark with a pencil where you will place each bucket shape. You might decide to stencil them randomly all over the quilt or

perhaps make a more ordered pattern of neat rows. Or how about stencilling a bucket border with several larger ones scattered across the middle?

4 Fix the main bucket and rim stencil in place with masking tape and then dab through a fabric paint using a stencil brush. Repeat across the quilt wherever you have decided to position the buckets. Change the colours as frequently as you like. Leave to dry.

5 Repeat with the handle and the bucket's contents stencils, leaving each colour to dry before stencilling on the next. Use a fresh stencil brush for each colour, or meticulously wash the brush in water between colours.

6 When all the colours are dry, iron on the back of the cover to fix the paints.

MAKING YOUR OWN QUILT COVER

To make a cover, simply use a sheet which when folded in half is large enough to cover a cot quilt. Fold it in half with right sides facing and stitch down the two long edges. Turn right sides out and stitch on stripey deckchair ties to close it up at the end. Then you can stencil your design on the front and back as described above.

Stencil 1 The main bucket and rim
Stencil 2 The handle
Stencil 3 The bucket's contents

STRAWBERRY FIELDS FOREVER

❤❤❤❤

An unusual but charming strawberry design adorns this pillowcase.
They are so life-like you can almost smell fresh strawberries.

MATERIALS

PILLOWCASE

ACETATE (3 PIECES)

PERMANENT MARKER

CRAFT KNIFE

CUTTING BOARD

MASKING TAPE

NEWSPAPER

FABRIC PAINTS (RED, GREEN, DARK GREEN, YELLOW)

STENCIL BRUSHES

MAKING A MATCHING QUILT AND PILLOWCASE

You needn't feel limited to stencilling these strawberries on to a pillowcase alone. A matching quilt would be great - see page 54 for instructions on making your own cover from sheeting. Similarly, the Sandy Buckets on page 54 could be used on a pillowcase - consider using just one bucket in a corner of the pillowcase to unite the two items in an understated way.

---

1 Trace and alter the size of the stencil given overleaf as appropriate (see page 9). Use one or both of the motifs, depending on your design needs. Transfer on to clear acetate and prepare the stencils as described on pages 10-11. For this design you will need three pieces of acetate:
● for the strawberry
● for the stalk and leaf
● for the pips.

2 Put a piece of newspaper between the layers of the pillowcase to prevent the paint passing through from the front to the back.

3 Use masking tape to keep the pillowcase flat and then mark with a pencil where you will place each strawberry.

4 Position the strawberry stencil and fix it in place with masking tape. Then dab through the red fabric paint and leave to dry.

5 Repeat with the stalk and leaf (using green and dark green, or just one colour if you prefer and the pips (using yellow) stencils, leaving each colour to try before stencilling the next. Use a fresh stencil brush for each colour, or meticulously wash the brush in water between colours.

6 When all the colours are dry, turn the pillow case inside out and carefully iron it on the back in order to fix the paints.

Stencil 1 The strawberry
Stencil 2 The stalk and leaf
Stencil 3 The pips

58

SWIMMING FISH

❤❤❤❤

You can buy plain wash bags or make your own from two squares of cotton lined with shower curtain fabric. The one here is made from yellow fabric and the paints are opaque which sit on the surface of the fabric so that the colour is not absorbed into the background.

MATERIALS

WASH BAG

ACETATE (3 PIECES)

PERMANENT MARKER

CRAFT KNIFE

CUTTING BOARD

MASKING TAPE

NEWSPAPER

FABRIC PAINTS (ORANGE, TURQUOISE, LIME GREEN, MAUVE)

STENCIL BRUSHES

COMBINING MOTIFS

There is such a wide choice of motifs in this book that you might decide to combine several elements from different designs to create something totally different. For example, you could design a charming underwater mural using the fish featured here, the starfish on page 88 and various - or all - of the elements of the Seaweed Surround on page 91. Simply add your own wave stencil, or indeed use the ones overleaf or on pages 16-17, to complete the mural.

---

1 Trace and alter the size of the stencil given overleaf as appropriate (see page 9). Use one or both of the motifs, depending on your design needs. Transfer on to clear acetate and prepare the stencils as described on pages 10-11. For this design you will need three pieces of acetate:
● for the fish's body and waves
● for the back fins
● for the eye, front fins and tail.

2 Fix the fabric in place with masking tape on a work surface covered with newspaper and then position the first piece of acetate in the centre to make the fish's body and waves, again fixing it with masking tape. Dab through the orange fabric paint for the body and the turquoise paint for the waves. Leave to dry. Use a fresh stencil brush for each colour, or meticulously wash the brush in water between colours.

3 Repeat for the other two stencil pieces. Use the lime green fabric paint for the back fins, and the mauve paint for the eye, front fins and tail. Leave each colour to dry before moving on to the next one.

4 When all the colours are dry, turn the bag over and carefully iron it on the back in order to fix the paints.

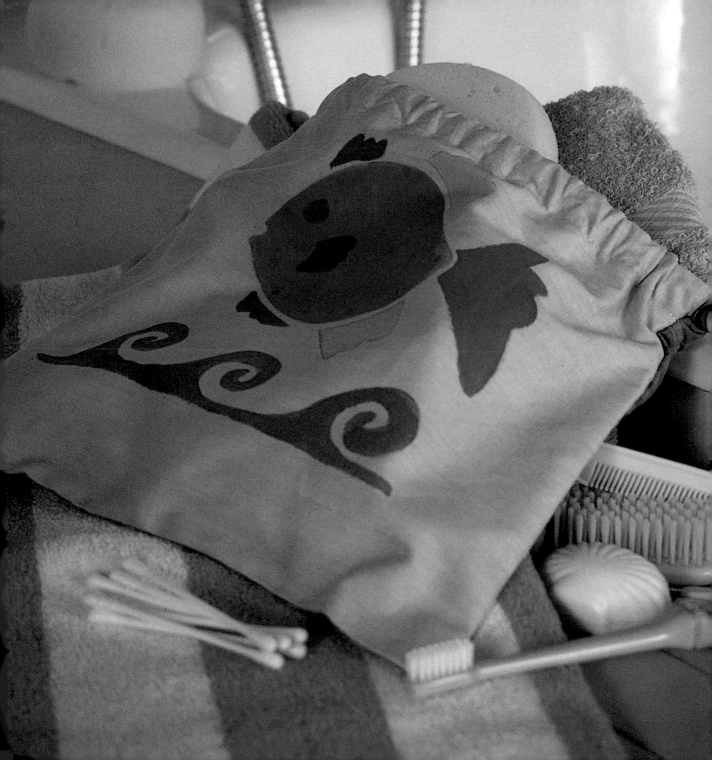

SNUFFLING PIG

♥♥♥♥

This jacket was decorated with images taken from the front cover of the book. The grass was traced from the front cover and cut out on acetate but the pig was enlarged (see page 9) before being traced on to acetate. The tufts of grass are a green pearl paint and the pig is a bright pink puff paint.

MATERIALS

JEANS JACKET

ACETATE (2 PIECES)

PERMANENT MARKER

CRAFT KNIFE

CUTTING BOARD

MASKING TAPE

NEWSPAPER

FABRIC FELT-TIPPED PENS (GREEN, PINK)

PEARLIZED PUFF PAINTS (GREEN, BRIGHT PINK)

STENCIL BRUSHES

1 Trace and alter the size of the grass and pig stencils given on the jacket as appropriate (see page 9). Put each motif on to a separate piece of acetate.

2 If you want to use the pig the same size as it appears on the jacket the stencil is ready-cut for you there. To prevent the paper from becoming too soggy with paint and so unusable, prepare it first with two coats of an oil-based paint.

3 Put a piece of newspaper in the centre of the jacket or open it out flat and use masking tape to fix it to a work surface.

4 First make the tufts of grass. Using masking tape to keep the stencil in place draw the grass outlines with the green fabric felt-tipped pen. Work around the border of the jacket until a complete grassy border is outlined. Then fill in each grass tuft shape using the green pearlized puff paint. Leave to dry.

5 Place the pig stencil on the centre back of the jacket and fix it in place with masking tape. Draw the outline with the pink fabric felt-tipped pen, as for the tufts of grass. Then remove the stencil and colour in the shape using the bright pink puff paint. Leave to dry.

6 When completely dry, iron on the back of the pig and the tufts of grass and the paint will then puff up very well.

STENCILLING EXTRA DECORATIONS

The small tufts of grass would look great repeated around the edge of the collar and/or the cuffs. And the pig could be but one of several snuffling on the back, with one or two pottering on the fronts.

SILHOUETTED RABBITS

❤❤❤❤

This mat has a stylized rabbit border design applied in black fabric paint to look like a silhouette.

MATERIALS

MAT IN PLAIN CLOSE WEAVE

ACETATE (1 PIECE)

PERMANENT MARKER

CRAFT KNIFE

CUTTING BOARD

MASKING TAPE

FABRIC FELT-TIPPED PEN (BLACK)

PAINTBRUSH

FABRIC PAINT (BLACK)

PAINTING A FLOOR

If your nursery has wooden floorboards these rabbits could also be stencilled around the edge of the room as a border reflecting the mat. Bright colours would certainly bring a lively atmosphere to the nursery.

Prepare the floor by thoroughly sanding the areas to be painted using a coarse sandpaper. Then you should very carefully measure and mark where each motif is to be stencilled. The more thoroughly you do this, the better the end result will be.

After you have finished the stencilling and left the paint to dry, apply two or three coats of varnish to seal both the stencils and the floorboards.

1 Trace and alter the size of the stencil given overleaf as appropriate (see page 9). Transfer on to clear acetate and prepare the stencil as described on pages 10-11. You will need only one piece of acetate for this design.

2 Use masking tape to keep the mat flat on a work surface and then mark with a pencil where you will place each rabbit motif.

3 Place the acetate on the mat where the first motif is to be stencilled and fix in place with masking tape.

4 Draw round the edge of the design using the black felt-tipped pen. Remove the stencil and repeat step 3 in the next position on the mat until the border has been completed.

5 Fill in the design using the paintbrush and the black fabric paint. You may, of course, stamp the paint through the stencil but it is easier to fill in a rough woven background by eye. The paint may seep under the edges of a stencil if it can't be applied close to a surface.

6 Leave to dry and then iron on the back of the mat to fix the fabric paint.

LITTLE BOATS

❤❤❤❤

These very pretty curtains are made from plain white sheeting on to which has been stencilled ice-cream coloured boats. As you can see, the design is not hard edged. Unlike many designs the slight splodginess of this one enhances rather than detracts from the overall look.

MATERIALS

WHITE FABRIC

ACETATE (3 PIECES)

PERMANENT MARKER

CRAFT KNIFE

CUTTING BOARD

MASKING TAPE

NEWSPAPER

FABRIC PAINTS (VARIOUS COLOURS)

STENCIL BRUSHES

FABRIC FELT-TIPPED PEN (BLACK) (OPTIONAL)

1 Trace and alter the size of the stencil given overleaf as appropriate (see page 9). Transfer on to clear acetate and prepare the stencils as described on pages 10-11. For this design you will need three pieces of acetate:
● for the blue elements
● for the deck, sails and wavy line
● for the central deck and stars.

The sheets (ropes) can be done on a separate piece of stencil acetate or they can be painted in freehand with a fabric felt- tipped pen later on. The latter is by far the easiest, but if you like cutting out stencils you may prefer to do it this way.

2 Fix the white fabric in place with masking tape on a work surface covered with newspaper and then mark with a pencil where you will position each boat.

3 Fix the first piece of acetate in place with masking tape and use blue fabric paint and a stencil brush to colour in the blue elements. I used different colours for each area but you might choose to limit your range. Use a fresh stencil brush for each colour, or meticulously wash the brush in water between colours.

4 Place the same stencil on the next position on the fabric, paint as before - but perhaps varying your choice of colours - and repeat until the first stencil is all over the fabric. Then leave to dry.

5 Place the second stencil in position and stencil over the first image. Repeat all over the fabric as in step 4.

6 Repeat steps 4 and 5 with the third stencil. Stencil or draw on the ropes. Leave to dry.

7 Iron on the back of the cloth to fix the design and then make up the curtains.

Stencil 1 The blue elements

Stencil 2 The deck, sails and wavy line

Stencil 3 The central deck and stars

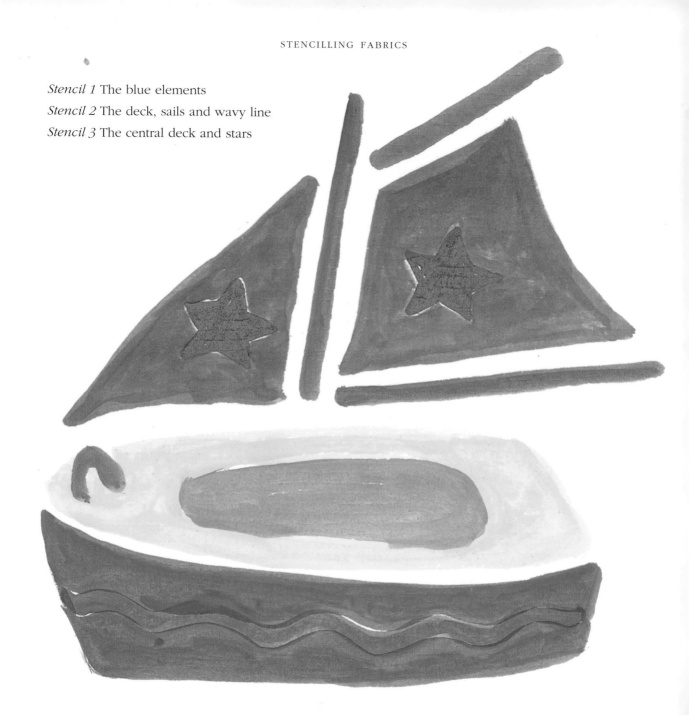

Stencilling
Accessories
♥♥♥

DUCKS AND DUCKLINGS

❤❤❤❤

This design is fairly simple and you can make it as long or as short as you need by adding or subtracting ducklings. The ducks and ducklings are stencilled using acrylic paints and the reedy grass is added later using oil crayons in green.

MATERIALS

WALL ON WHICH TO STENCIL MURAL
ACETATE (4 PIECES)
PERMANENT MARKER
CRAFT KNIFE
CUTTING BOARD
MASKING TAPE
ACRYLIC PAINTS (WHITE, YELLOW, ORANGE, BLUE)
STENCIL BRUSHES
FELT-TIPPED (BLACK) PEN
STENCIL CRAYON (GREEN)

1 Trace and alter the size of the stencils given overleaf and on page 78 as appropriate (see page 9). Transfer them on to clear acetate and prepare the stencils as described on pages 10-11. For this design you will need to prepare four pieces of acetate:
● for the duck body
● for the duckling body
● for the duckling wings, beak and feet
● for the grass.

2 Fix the duck body to the wall using masking tape to hold the stencil in place. Using the white acrylic paint, make the mother duck's body and use yellow for the beak and feet. Then move the stencil to make the father duck, this time using orange acrylic paint for the beak and feet. Use a fresh stencil brush for each colour, or meticulously wash the brush in water between colours.

3 Stencil the bodies of the ducklings in yellow followed by their wings, beaks and feet (using the orange acrylic paint).

4 Finally add all the eyes by hand using the black felt-tipped pen.

5 Next stencil in the grass using the stencil crayon. Rub the stencil crayon on to a spare piece of acetate to get a piece of colour. Then pick up some of the colour on a stencil brush and, carefully holding the stencil with your fingers, dab the colour off the brush through the stencil on to the wall. Slowly work around the ducks, using different amounts of pressure to make sure the grass looks lighter in some places than others. Also change the angle of the stencil as you go.

6 Sponge blue acrylic paint between the grass to look like water.

Stencil 1 The duck body

Stencil 2 The duckling body

Stencil 3 The duckling wings, beak and feet

Stencil 4 The grass

CHEEKY CAT

♥♥♥♥

This plate has been decorated using a stencil and ceramic paints. Although hard wearing, these paints are not really suitable for everyday use, so the plate is to hang on the wall.

MATERIALS

PLAIN CERAMIC PLATE

ACETATE (4 PIECES)

PERMANENT MARKER

CRAFT KNIFE

CUTTING BOARD

MASKING TAPE

CERAMIC PAINTS (TURQUOISE, YELLOW, MAUVE, PURPLE)

STENCIL BRUSHES

TURPENTINE

Note: Ceramic paints will take at least 24 hours to dry and sometimes longer.

VARYING THE DESIGN

You can, of course, customize the colour of this cat to match your own or a friend's cat. Make an additional stencil (or stencils) for the markings and lay this over the basic outline painted in the lightest colour. The paw marks, too, can be painted to match.

---

1 Trace and alter the size of the stencil given overleaf as appropriate (see page 9). Use as many or the paw prints as you need for your design. Transfer on to clear acetate and prepare the stencils as described on pages 10-11. For this design you will need four pieces of acetate:
● for the cat's face
● for the whiskers
● for the ears, eyes and nose
● for the paws.

2 Position the cat's face stencil in the centre of the plate and fix in place with masking tape. Using the paint fairly dry, stencil through the turquoise ceramic paint. Leave to dry.

3 Stencil the cat's whiskers using yellow ceramic paint. Leave to dry and then stencil the ears, eyes and nose. If you like, make the eyes a different colour to that of the ears and nose. I used purple for the eyes and mauve for the other features. Use a fresh stencil brush for each colour, or meticulously wash the brush in turpentine between colours.

4 Use the purple to stencil some paw prints round the rim of the plate leaving space for alternate coloured paw marks.

5 Wipe the paw print stencil clean with a cloth dipped in turpentine and then dry it. Stencil yellow paw prints round the rim of the plate between the purple ones.

Stencil 1 The cat's face

Stencil 2 The whiskers

Stencil 3 The ears, eyes and nose

Stencil 4 The paws

HAREING AROUND

❤❤❤❤

The hare motif has been taken from the back cover of this book. It has been stencilled around a ceramic wall lamp and reduced to decorate a peg board.

MATERIALS

WOODEN PEG BOARD

WALL LIGHT

SANDPAPER (FINE GRADE)

WOOD PRIMER

PAINTBRUSH

UNDERCOAT

EMULSION PAINTS (BLUE, GREEN, PALE YELLOW)

SPONGE

ACETATE (1 PIECE)

PERMANENT MARKER

CRAFT KNIFE

CUTTING BOARD

MASKING TAPE

STENCIL CRAYON (BROWN)

STENCIL BRUSHES

FELT-TIPPED PENS (BLACK, BROWN)

TURPENTINE

CLEAR POLYURETHANE VARNISH

THE PEG BOARD

1 Prepare the peg board by rubbing it down with the sandpaper, then paint with wood primer and leave to dry. Paint with undercoat and leave to dry. Finally, paint the top half of the board with pale blue emulsion paint and leave to dry.

2 Paint the bottom half and the pegs with a slightly darker green. When paint is dry,

sponge over the top with a darker green.

3 Trace and alter the size of the hare stencil given on the jacket as appropriate (see page 9). Transfer on to clear acetate and prepare the stencil as described on pages 10-11.

4 If you want to use the hare the same size as it appears on the jacket, the stencil is ready-cut. To prevent the paper from becoming too soggy, prepare it with two coats of an oil-based paint first.

5 Position the stencil over the pegs as in the photograph opposite, fixing it in place with masking tape.

6 Paint the hares with brown stencil crayon and mark the eyes with a black felt-tipped pen.

7 Leave the colours to set which will take about three days. Once dry, paint the board with a coat of clear polyurethane varnish.

THE WALL LIGHT

1 Paint the wall light with pale yellow emulsion and when dry sponge green round the base of the light as you did for the peg board.

2 Prepare your stencil as above and position the stencil on the light, fixing it in place with masking tape. Draw around the stencil with a pencil, remove it and fill in the body with the brown felt-tipped pen. Then mark the eyes of the hare with the black felt-tipped pen.

WIND IN THE WILLOWS

❤❤❤❤

This design was inspired by The Wind in the Willows *and includes water, ducks, reeds, bulrushes and a frog.*

MATERIALS

PAPER FOR BORDER OR FRIEZE

ACETATE (2 PIECES)

PERMANENT MARKER

CRAFT KNIFE

CUTTING BOARD

MASKING TAPE

TAPE MEASURE OR RULER

STENCIL CRAYONS (BROWNS, GREENS, BLUE)

STENCIL BRUSHES

TURPENTINE

1 Trace and alter the size of the stencils given overleaf as appropriate (see page 9). Transfer on to clear acetate and prepare the stencils as described on pages 10-11. For this design you will need two pieces of acetate:
● for the main part of the design
● for the details (beak, feet, bulrushes).

2 Position the first stencil on to the paper or part of the wall you wish to stencil, fixing it in place with masking tape.

3 Rub the first stencil crayon on to a spare piece of acetate to get a piece of colour. Pick up some of the colour on a stencil brush and then carefully, holding the stencil with your fingers, dab the colour off the brush through the stencil on to the paper or wall.

4 When the first colour is applied, put on the other colours one by one. For this design you will need to use a fresh brush for each colour, or meticulously wash the brush in turpentine between colours. Leave to dry and repeat as necessary along the paper or around the wall.

5 Place the second stencil over the top of the first piece of stencilling, making sure you align all the parts of the design. Apply the next colours, as before. The texture of the brush will give a soft and authentic look to the feathers and bulrushes. For a more lifelike look, mix the colours (see below).

6 When finished, wash the brushes in turpentine. The design will take about three days to set.

ADDING TEXTURE

The stencilling on this design has deliberately been made to look more textured. This is easy to do. After stencilling the base colours, stipple a light coating of a contrasting colour - or more if you wish to enhance the effect still further - across the top keeping the stencil in place.

For a three-dimensional effect, add darker colours around the edge of a motif on just one side. This will give it the illusion of depth and added interest.

Stencil 1 The main part of the design

Stencil 2 The details (beak, feet, bulrushes)

BRIGHT STARFISH

❤❤❤❤

You can decorate plain white tiles to coordinate with your child's or baby's bathroom. I used a simple starfish design in orange and yellow. The paints are specially made for use on glazed ceramics. They are reasonably hard wearing but may be further protected with varnish.

MATERIALS

PLAIN CERAMIC TILES

ACETATE (2 PIECES)

PERMANENT MARKER

CRAFT KNIFE

CUTTING BOARD

MASKING TAPE

CERAMIC PAINTS (YELLOW, ORANGE)

STENCIL BRUSHES

TURPENTINE

CLEAR POLYURETHANE VARNISH

Note: Ceramic paints will take at least 24 hours to dry and sometimes longer.

VARYING THE DESIGN

Don't just stick to these starfish for decorating bathroom tiles. Think about adding other fishy motifs, such as the shells and fish featured on page 90 of this book. A huge octopus across a number of tiles with tentacles reaching out to other motifs would be pretty dramatic. Look through books and magazines to glean ideas for your designs - stencilling is all about using your imagination.

1 Trace and alter the size of the stencil given overleaf as appropriate (see page 9). Use one or several starfish, depending on your design needs. Transfer on to clear acetate and prepare the stencils as described on pages 10-11. For this design, you will need two pieces of acetate:
● for the starfish outline
● for the details.

2 Position the starfish outline stencil on to one of the tiles and fix in place with masking tape. Using the paint fairly dry, stencil a yellow star.

3 Use the same colour to stencil further tiles and leave them all to dry. Turn the stencil around a little each time you stencil a new starfish. This will prevent the overall look of the tiles from becoming too rigid.

4 Wipe the stencil with a cloth dipped in turpentine and then dry it. Stencil further tiles in orange. Leave all the tiles to dry. Use a fresh stencil brush for each colour, or meticulously wash the brush in turpentine between colours.

5 Use the second stencil to stencil on the dotted details. Use orange on the yellow stars and yellow on the orange stars. Leave to set for about three days.

Stencil 1 The starfish outline

Stencil 2 The details

SEAWEED SURROUND

♥♥♥♥

This wall surround is based on seaweed tendrils to fit in with a pretty cottage bedroom. The soft colours are similar to those used in the Litle Boat curtains (see page 69).

MATERIALS

WALL

ACETATE (2 PIECES)

PERMANENT MARKER

CRAFT KNIFE

CUTTING BOARD

MASKING TAPE

STENCIL CRAYONS (VARIOUS COLOURS)

STENCIL BRUSHES

TURPENTINE

PLANNING A BORDER

Before stencilling a border, whether it be around a window, room or floor, thoroughly plan it out, particularly the corner turns. Make a scaled plan on squared paper and then sketch in your ideas. Do make sure that your measurements are accurate so that when it comes to transferring the design to the surface to be painted you won't suddenly find it is going wrong.

---

1 Trace and alter the size of the stencils given overleaf and on page 94 as appropriate (see page 9). Transfer on to clear acetate and prepare the stencil as described on pages 10-11. For this design, you will need two pieces of acetate:
● for the window surround
● for the fish, starfish and shell details.

2 Position the window surround stencil on the wall where you wish the design to start. Fix in place with masking tape.

3 Using the stencil crayons, colour in the seaweed, starfish and shell with whatever colours you choose. This might depend on what colours you already have or the colour of the existing decor.

4 Repeat the motif as many times as necessary to complete your surround. Leave to dry. Use a fresh stencil brush for each colour, or meticulously wash the brush in turpentine between colours.

5 Place the second stencil over the surround and stencil in all the markings using darker or contrasting colours over the existing shades.

6 Leave the colours to set which will take about three days.

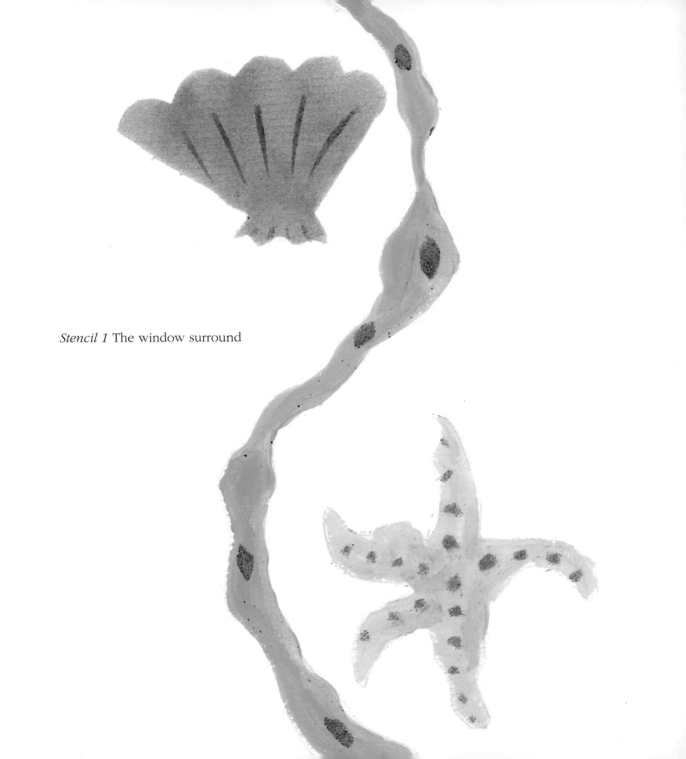

Stencil 1 The window surround

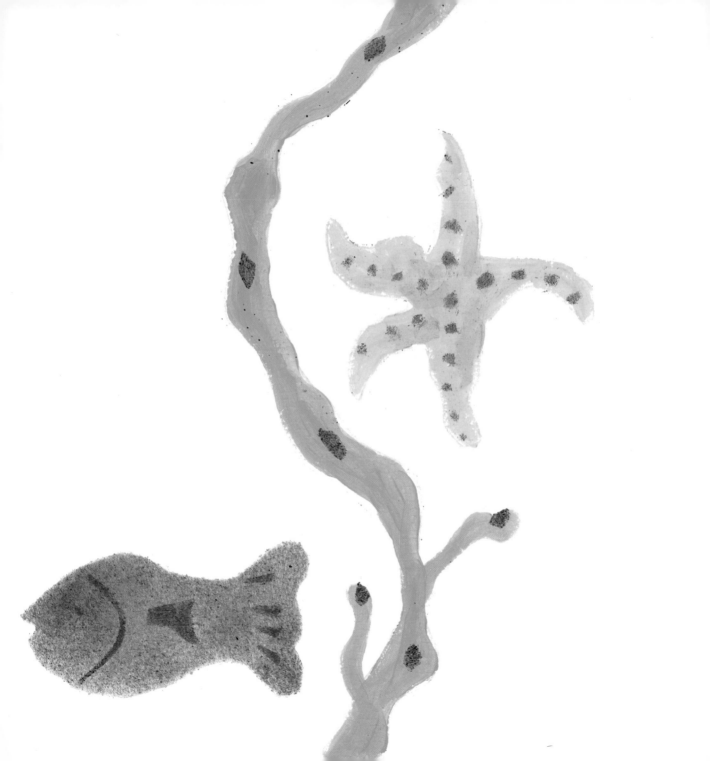

Stencil 2 The fish, starfish and shell details

94

STOCKISTS AND ACKNOWLEDGMENTS

The author and publishers would like to thank the following suppliers for their generosity:

Phillip and Tacey Ltd
North Way
Andover
SP10 5BA
for supplying Pebeo, fabric pens, ceramic paints and acrylic colours.

Eurostudio Ltd
Unit 4
Southdown Industrial Estate
Southdown Road
Harpenden
Herts AL5 1PW
for supplying stencil crayons, acetate, stencil brushes.

MFI Furniture Centres Ltd
Southon House
333 The Hyde
Edgeware Rd
Colindale
London NW9 6TD
for supplying the blanket box, coffee table, sheet and pillowcase.

Dylon International Ltd
Worsley Bridge Road
Lower Sydenham
London SE26 5HD
for supplying fabric paints, pens and puff paints.

Inscribe
Borden
Hants
for supplying tulip puff, glitter and pearl paints.

Gloriana Page for kindly allowing me to decorate her daughter's cot.

Many thanks to Marie-Lou Avery for making and creating wonderful photographs. Gloria Nicol with her unerring sense of style and design for choosing the props. Emma Callery for sorting out my manuscript always with humour. Petra Boase for designing and printing many of the items in the book. To Denise Bates who asked me to write it.